MOUNTAIN MOVER

I0154369

EILEEN CURTEIS

CCB Publishing
British Columbia, Canada

Mountain Mover

Copyright ©2019 by Eileen Curteis
ISBN-13   978-1-77143-401-0
First Edition

Library and Archives Canada Cataloguing in Publication
Curteis, Eileen, 1942-, author
Mountain mover / written and illustrated by Eileen Curteis. -- First edition.
Issued in print and electronic formats.
ISBN 978-1-77143-401-0 (softcover).--ISBN 978-1-77143-402-7 (PDF)
Additional cataloguing data available from Library and Archives Canada

Cover artwork and interior pastel drawings and collages,
as well as all poems are by Eileen Curteis.

Cover design by Carey Pallister.

Author photo credit: Barbara Benedetti

Publisher: CCB Publishing
               British Columbia, Canada
               www.ccbpublishing.com

I serve a God who is my mountain mover.
Mark 11, 23.

Written for my friends

who travel the journey with me.

Acknowledgement

Carey Pallister, Province Archivist for the Sisters of Saint Ann, deserves recognition for her editorial and digital skills, for her artistic arrangement of my book, and for her great generosity in helping me put this manuscript together.

PREFACE

Mountain Mover invites you to go on a journey inward. It says to its travellers that in all of life's hazards there is a summit worth struggling for.

Mountain Mover could be anyone of any race or creed. It doesn't really matter who we are when the hardships of life come knocking at our door.

You might say we were given a key at birth to unlock our destiny. If that is so, why then does it take a lifetime for us weary travellers to get there? Perhaps it's because life is a sacred journey upward and for the climber who is ascending the mountain he or she doesn't always know that.

The poetry and art in this book speak about the reality of struggle that is found in all our lives. It's the distasteful part of the journey we would like to avoid and, yet, to arrive at the summit of our dreams we must walk through the land of the dismal to get there.

Beauty is something we all strive for and *Mountain Mover* assures us that it is our Divine birthright to attain it.

Eileen Curteis, ssa

SOARING HIGH

I am
a complex bird
grief grown
and flying high.
I am
the yellow winged
one
sailing through
the dark
of night.
Sometimes
lost and bewildered
I know
Infinity
is the home
I go to.

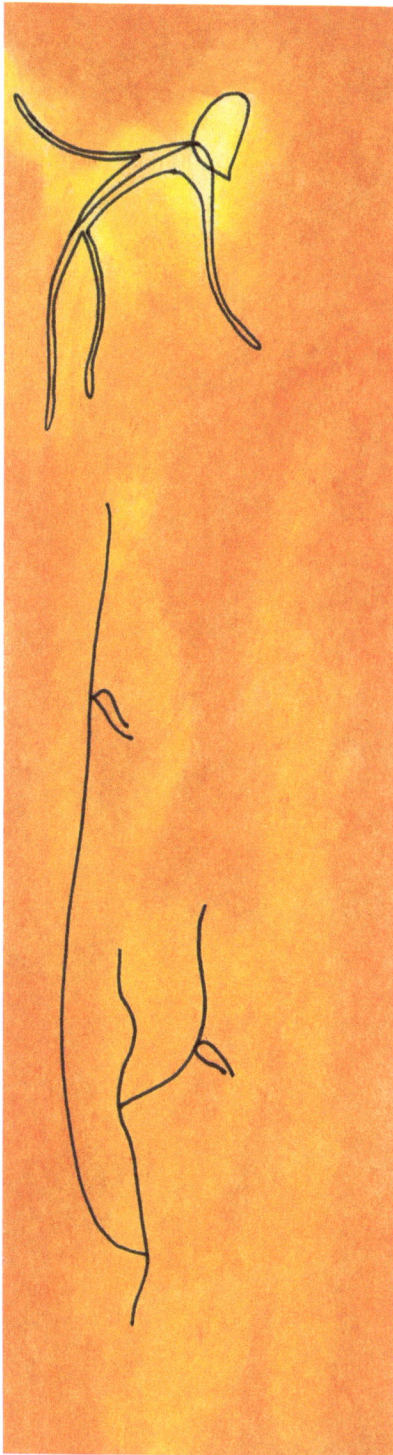

MOMENTARY ANNIHILATION

It was something phenomenal
this fear
that was mounting
inside her, now,
something
like the devastation
of an earthquake
when there wasn't one
and that is why,
she said,
the risk
of losing one's purpose
is as terrifying
as it is.

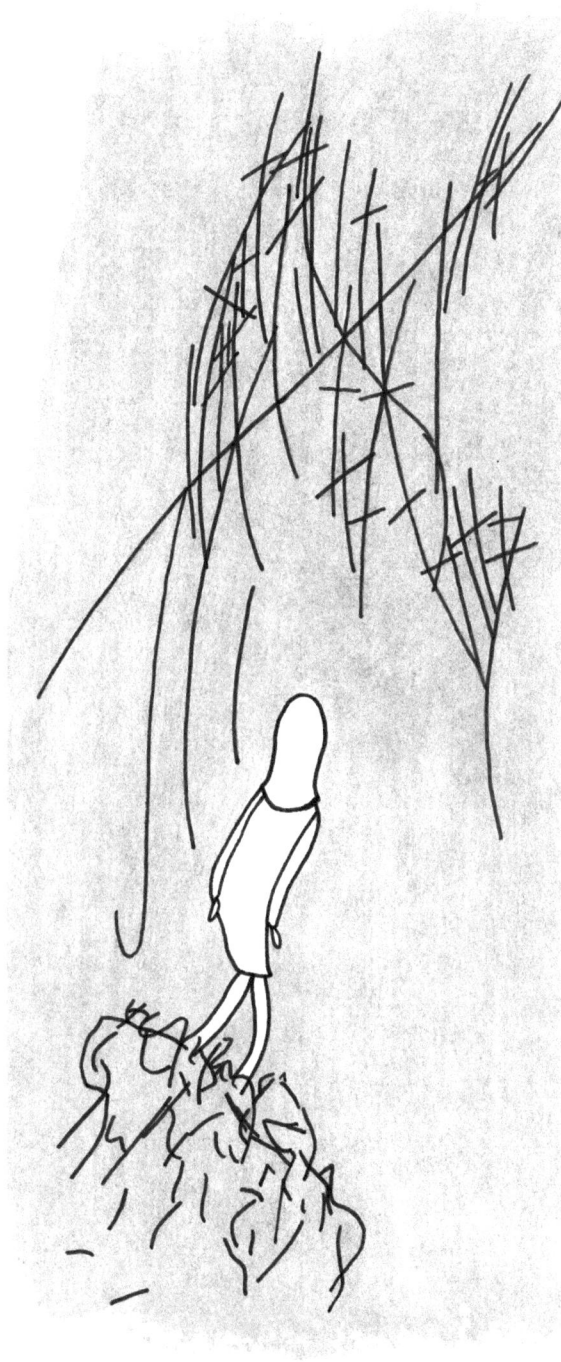

RAGGED RUNNER

If deceit
is what
you eradicate
then you are
a winner
so be true
to yourself
marathon runner-
elicit joy
from defeat
and run
as though
your life
depended
on it.

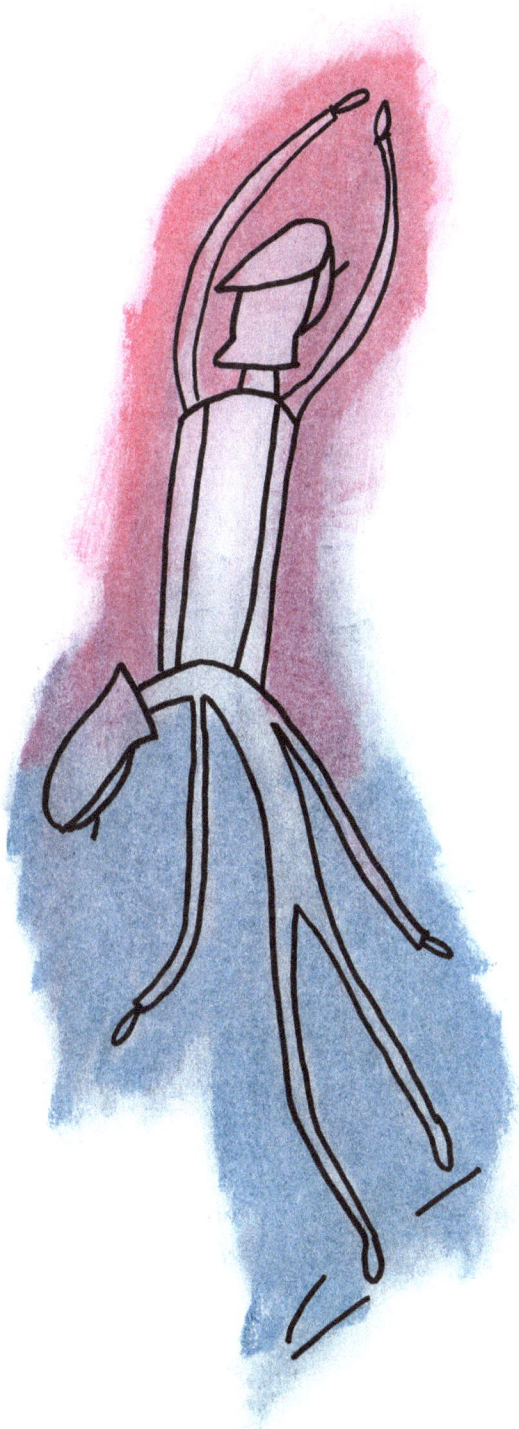

BROKEN OPEN

Knocked over
struck down
by a boulder
she could have been
a skeleton
hanging
in mid air
because this time
she saw
more vividly
than ever
how the harshness
of life
strips you open
leaves you naked
leaves you bare.

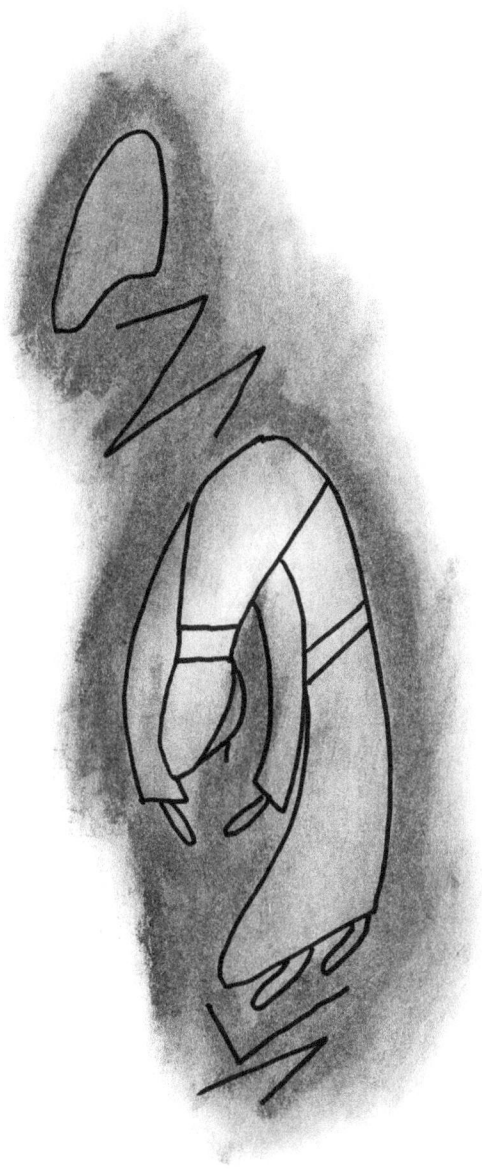

YIELDED

The time will come
when you must leave
this valley.
Think not upon it
but when the time comes
know
that it must be so.
Leave that which you love
and are accustomed to
and though it breaks
your heart
do not wish it otherwise.
Follow Him in darkness
unto Light.
Bear with bitterness
know
that it is but the pulp
of tommorow's fruit.

NEW FACE
OF GOD

When the two feet
of a bird
and a woman
get cut off
in midlife
they don't lose
their song
entirely.
They just go
searching
for a new God
more colourful
than the narrow
limiting
old faced one
of the past.

TRANSFORMING POWER

In the time
of destruction
I shall make
my way
inside
your rudderless
body.
I shall say to you:
Receive
this lighthouse
in memory
of your
ruined self
then as a beacon
conceal it
from no one!

PUSHING FORWARD

If God's voice
said:
stop clinging
to a wobbly stool
your feet
were made
to travel
elsewhere
she would do it
and yet,
hanging on
to her stationary
position
was something
she could not
immediately
let go of.

WIND
DAUGHTER

You run
with the wind
as though
he were your brother
and you say to him—
Oh sister, mother,
father, brother,
must I
like the breeze
be bent
to the grief
I carry
and you in answer
said to me—
When you have
been bent freely
then shall you rise
above it
and all
will be well again.

SELF RECOVERY

Sometimes
the only identity
I have
gets stampeded
out of me
and I hear
somewhere
off
in the distance
the tragic whisper
in the mouth
of a blackbird
say:
it is the recovery
of your own self
you long for.

WHOLESOME SHIPWRECK

In the attainment
of beauty
some say
you were destined
for shipwreck—
that in good weather
or bad
it was bound to come
and that being driven
by the false current
of a mighty wind
was your way
of arriving
at the finish line.

FLYING FREE

Embracing
the freedom
of a kite
within her
would eventually
lead her
to say:
I am coming out
of the safe box
of rectangular
living
where flattened
people
become whole
again.

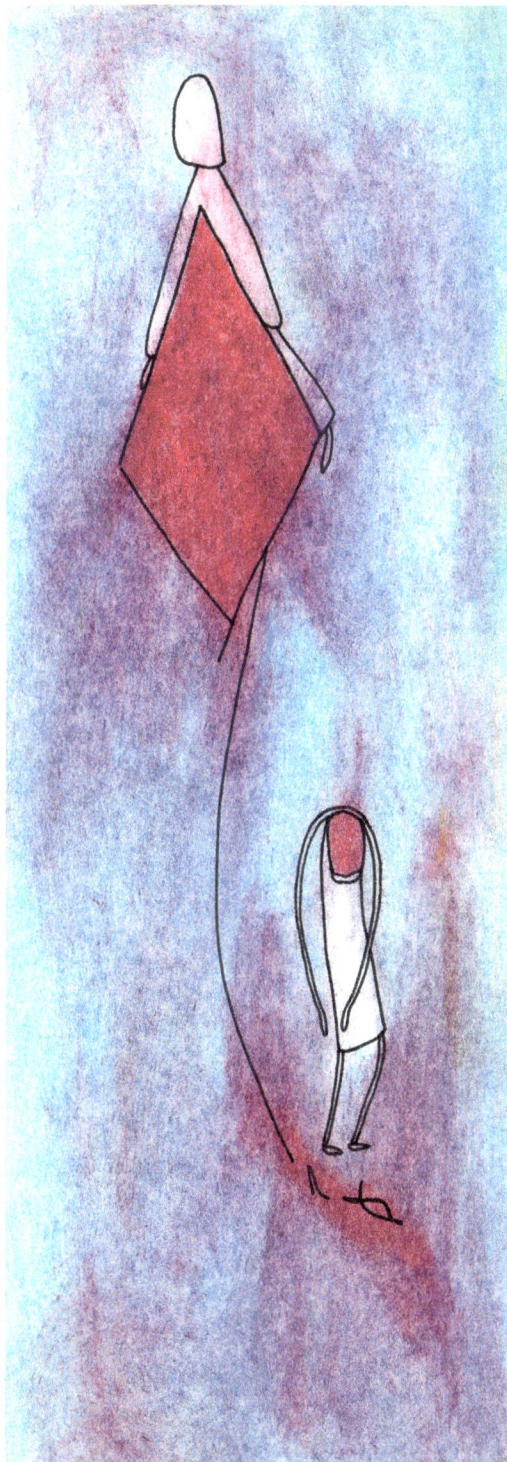

CLEAN VESSEL

Falling
into a deep stupor
she said to her Maker:
"In the ground of my being
weeds
are something
I suffer from
so when you wash
the hardened part
of my clay
clean
remove from me
the shame
of how
I got to be
that way."

DETERMINED CLIMBER

How difficult it is
to change
the mute face
of a strong mountain
and, yet,
with determination
she knew
she could do it.
Even
if it took
a lifetime
to discover
whether it was
her face or God's face
she was after
didn't really matter
just so long as she found
what she was looking for.

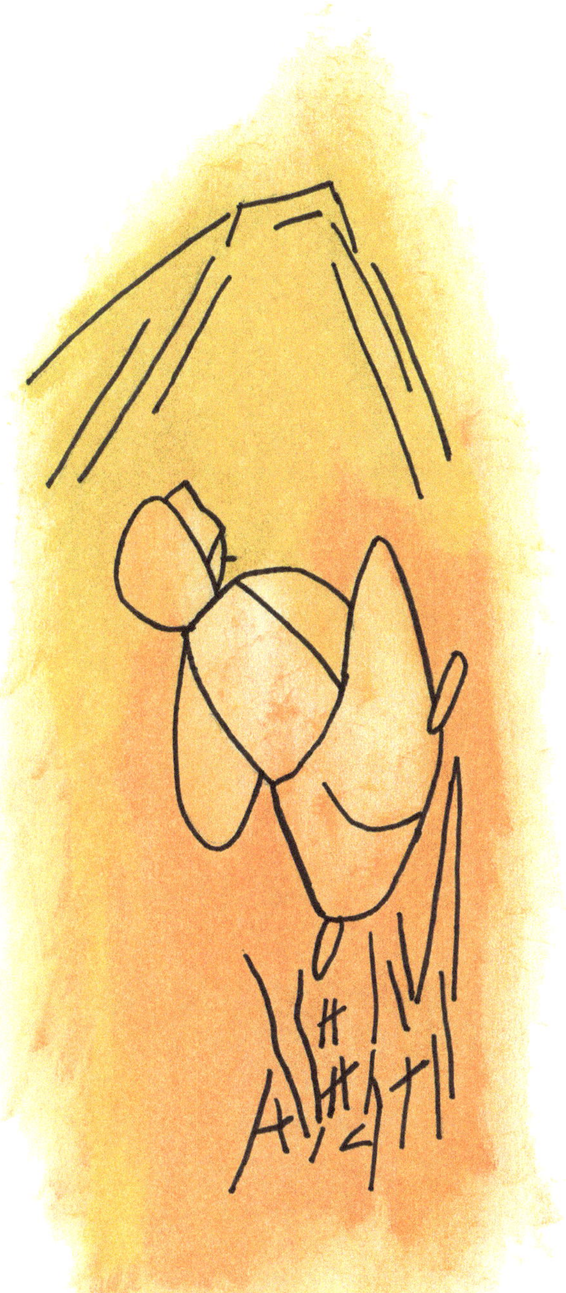

STAIRWAY
TO GOD

Even the smallest
glimmer of God
was enough
to send her
on her way
and, yet,
as much
as she longed
for the day
when freedom
would come
hidden
in her body
were these
insurmountable
stairs
hurdles
of every kind
to climb up
over
and through.

HARD FALL

Gaze gently
on the soil
of your
inner self.
Look kindly
on the way
you fell.
Then enter into
these regions
and know
in all sincerity
that if it were
weakness only
that put you here
you would not now
have attained
the strength
it takes
to be respectable.

UNLEASHING THE SELF

Strapped down
straddled in
how did I get
to be this way?
Somebody
set the trap
and I
stepped into it.
It's incumbent now
that I release
myself
from this
barbed wire
entanglement.

BREAKING
LOOSE

Not only
do I long
for the birds
of Spring
in my own life
but for the realization
of it
in the lives of others too
for what is beauty
one's own
or anyone else's
lest it find
fuller expression
within the cages
of our silent
cramped in hearts
who must learn
that to fly
is not a bad thing.

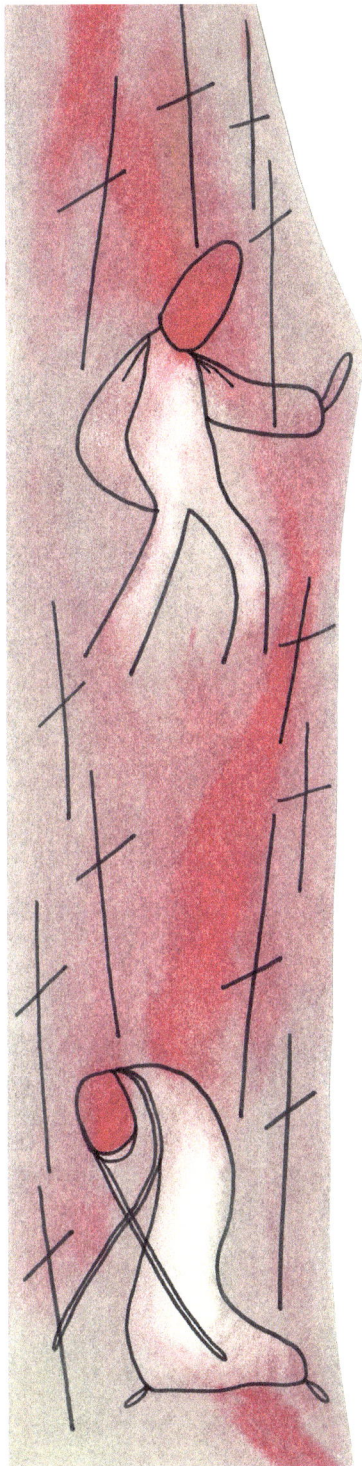

FRAGILE
BEAUTY

She was adept
at falling
but the desire
to climb
had always
been in her
and, so,
she went forward
as a
breakable figure
with a strong kind
of fragility
admitting to herself
and everyone
that the effortless way
of walking
had never
been easy.

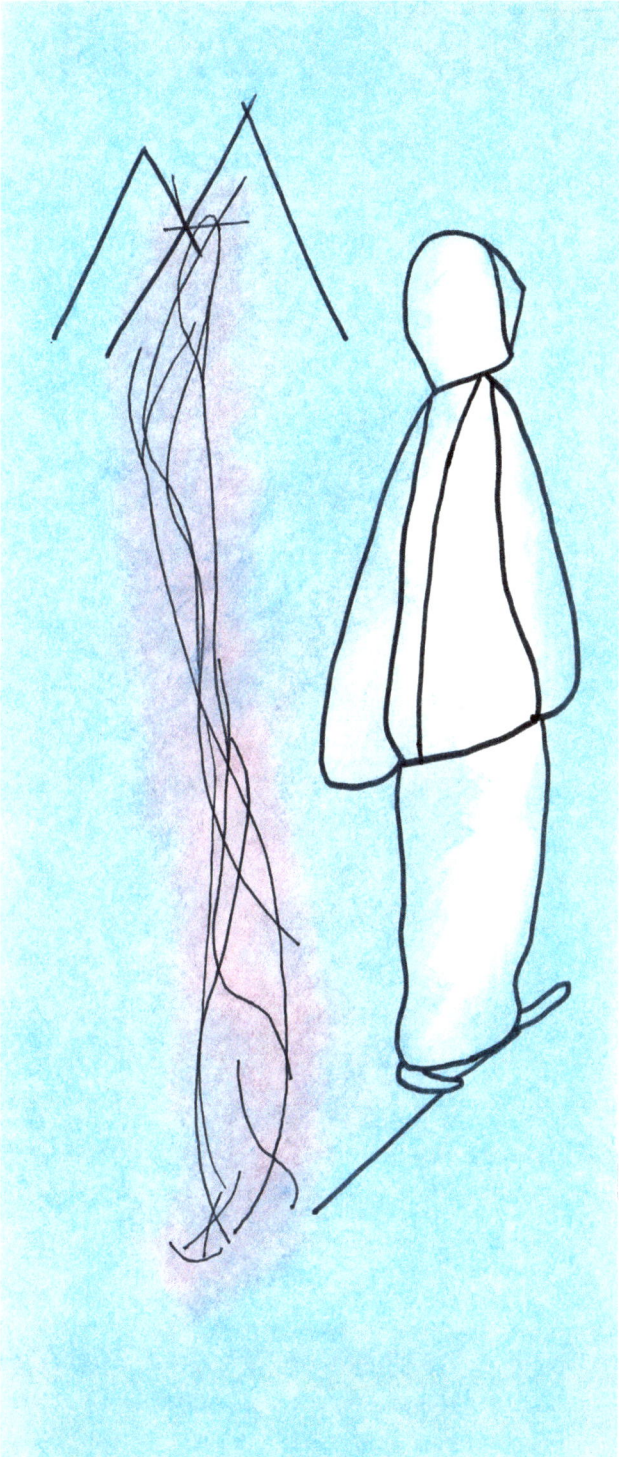

FIRE WOMAN

The pain
of experience
taught her
that nobody
likes
getting burnt
and, yet,
being burnt
was a part
of her progression,
she said,
the necessary part
that nobody
could save her from.

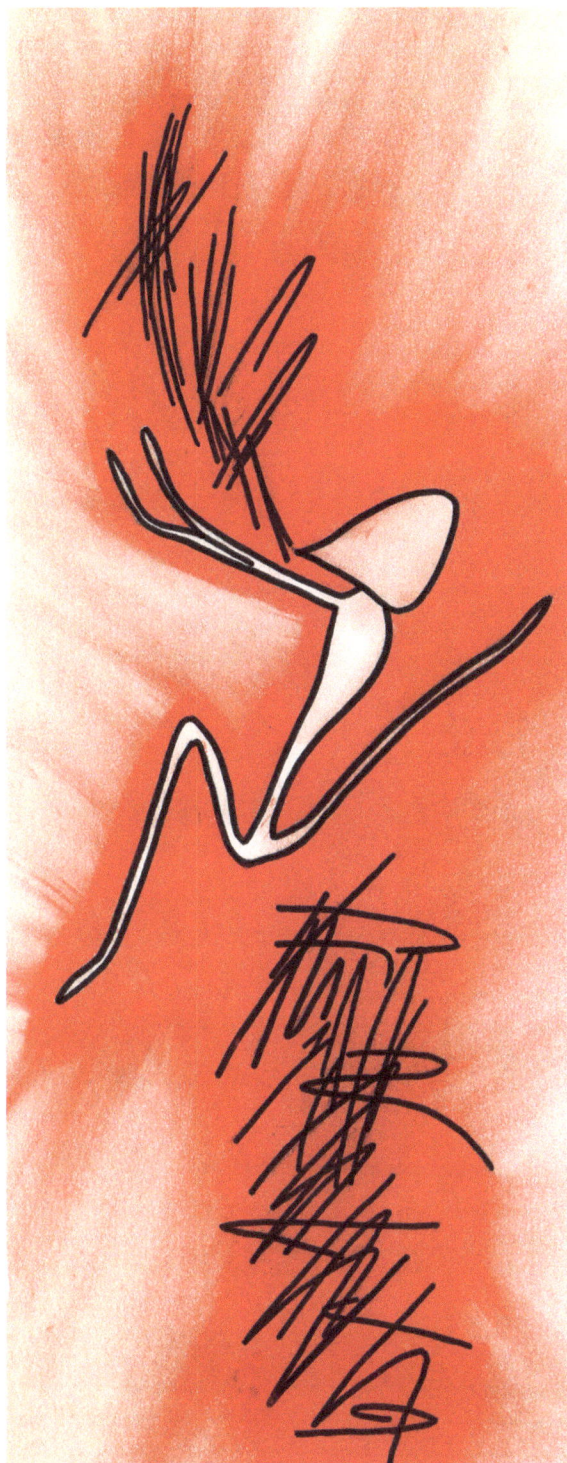

MOUNTAIN MOVER

To have sat
with the soul
in terrifying
weakness
and to have made
the discovery
that there is
no moving
of mountains
except
in moments
like these.

Mountain
Mover
1977

SUN HEALER

Coming out of
her worst
devastation
she was able
to say:
It was worth
waiting for
because
what she found
in this Friend
was a love
that could
penetrate her
like the warmth
of the sun
and no one
had ever done that
for her.

STRONG WOMAN

When the cruel face
of destruction
slaps you
hard enough
how important
it is
to carry
within you
the serenity
of God
and how strong
you really
have to be
to preserve yourself
in gentleness.

1977
Woman

MOUNTAIN SUNRISE

If she waited
on top
of a mountain
she would never
get
to the sunrise
and so,
she began
at the beginning
of the barrier
that was herself
and slowly
worked her way up
through each
of the prohibitions.

THE HUMAN HEARTBEAT

When she
had moved beyond
the state
of being
an anonymous person
not only
did she see
the beauty
in herself
and others
but she also saw
that if
she desired love
it was because
the craving
of humanity
was in her.

MY CREED

I believe in You
though you colour
my heaven black.
I believe in You
though you blot out
the sun from my sky
I believe in You
though people
laugh at me
for my belief
and I shall go on
believing
because having
believed once
I have naught
else to do.

STORM LOVER

If ultimate growth means
placing myself
in immediate contact
with a storm
that will chisel me
then I will place myself
in immediate contact
with a storm
that will chisel me.

And if the rocks
of the earth
shall hurl me downward
I will say:
out of rock I was formed
and out of rock I will climb
to the extremities
of a landscape
where I can be hoisted
to You.

FINAL DELIVERY

For this kind
of an enemy
the only way
to rout it
was with the truth
and that is why
it took
a brutal kind
of self knowledge
that led her to say
if I am
a hidden tree
of despair
I cannot deny it
any longer
or it will deny me
and for years
that is what
she had been doing.

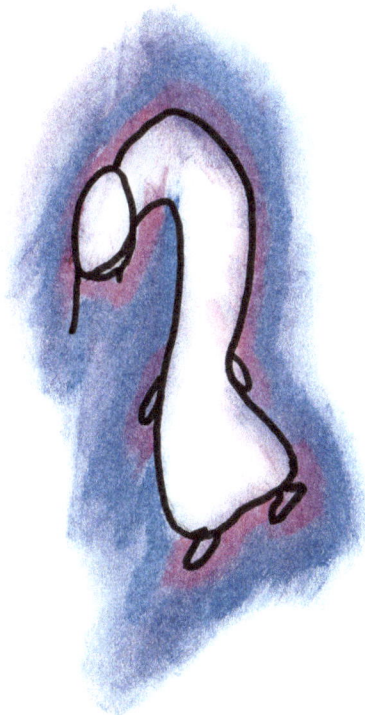

THE THORNY TRUTH

Burying
her grief
it went
deep down
deeper still
until
her punctured heart
cried out:
If being pierced
by the thorn
of a rose
creates blood
on my finger
then I want
no more of it!

CAREFUL WALKER

If she was
the gentle
strong one
she would have to
rediscover it
for herself
and, so,
she was being careful
of the ground
on which she walked
because she needed
the time
and space,
she said,
never to be destroyed
again
by the evil
of too much pressure.

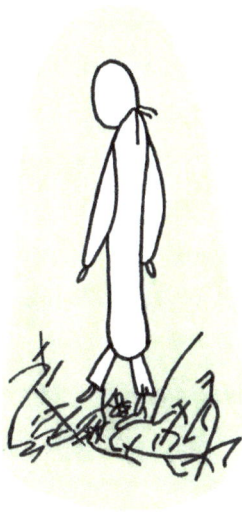

BLIND JOURNEY

It was a persistent Voice
that said—
Believe in Me still more
and never question
the deviousness of the route
for I have always been there
as the reward
of your following.
Her experience
past and present
had taught her this
but it did not alter the fact
that this blind striving
of going nowhere
when she definitely wanted
to be going somewhere
was like cutting off
the hands of a person,
her person,
which made the promise
of renewal
all the more difficult.

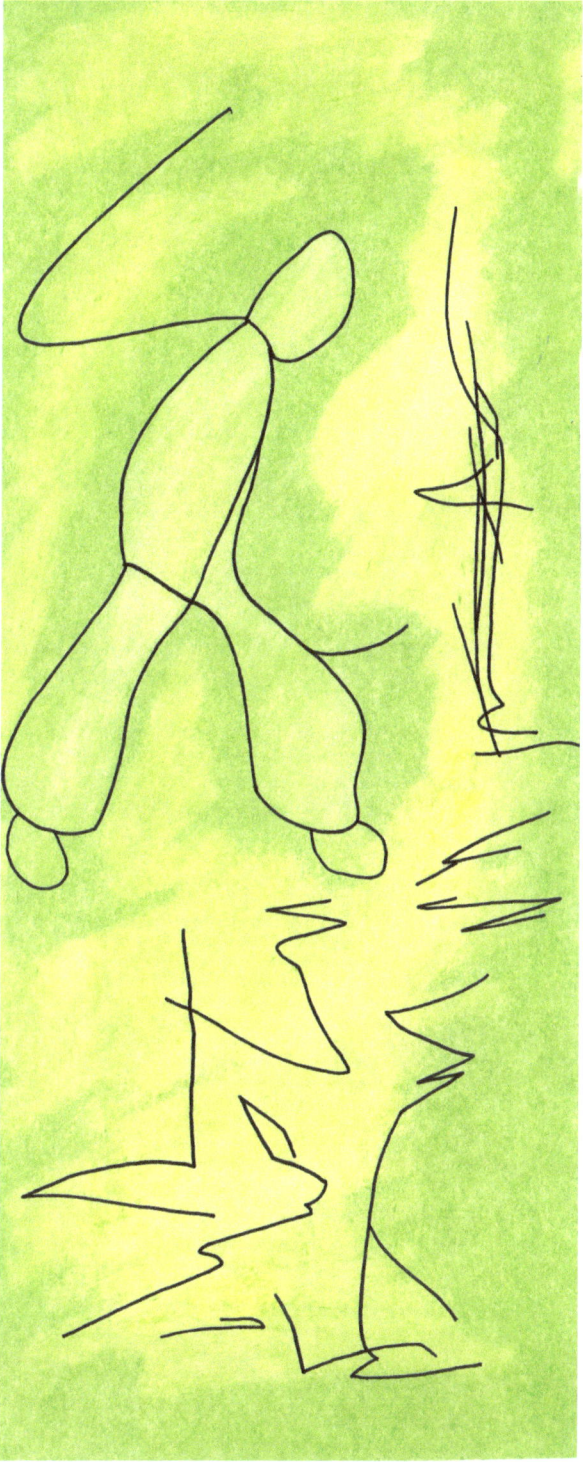

CLIMBING UPWARD

Collapsing
under a mountain
of despair
it's never easy
trudging uphill
to where
the Life Force is
but once
you've done it,
she said,
there's no
turning back.

THE QUESTIONER

Without answers
she was beginning
to question
if this person
she called God
had a voice
and did He
really speak to her
or was it just a figment
of her imagination?
Of course,
she knew He existed
but momentarily
she had lost her way
and if ever
she needed friends
it was now
in this period of doubt.

RAIN CHILD

In the slow
drizzle
of this rain
she caught
a glimpse
of her soul
and though
she had said
she did not like
to be
melancholy
she knew
that over the years
there were
these streaks
of sadness
in her.

SALVIFIC HEALING

I believe in scorched hearts
and broken limbs,
in blood
and in people,
but most of all
I believe in delivery from them
or to put it
another way,
I believe
that we cannot bring death
into the life
of a person
without first promising
some kind of a healing.

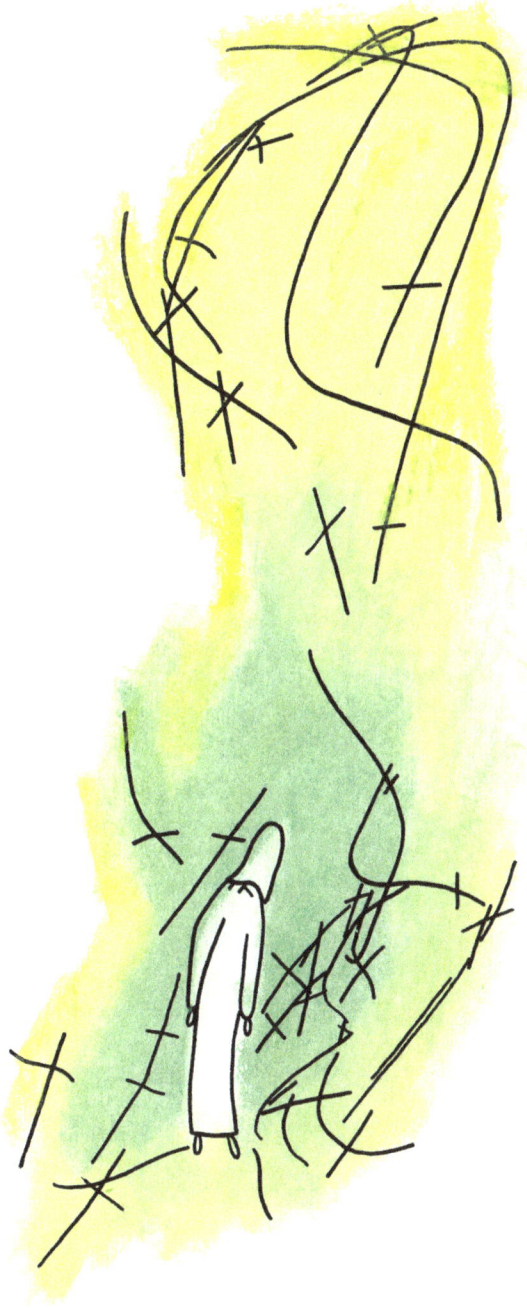

COSTLY FORMATION

Whether it was
the evil
of a fiery serpent
or the eruption
of darkness
in her
she didn't know
what could be
worse
than this
and, yet,
in the process
of becoming
beautiful
it was something
she had to
pass through.

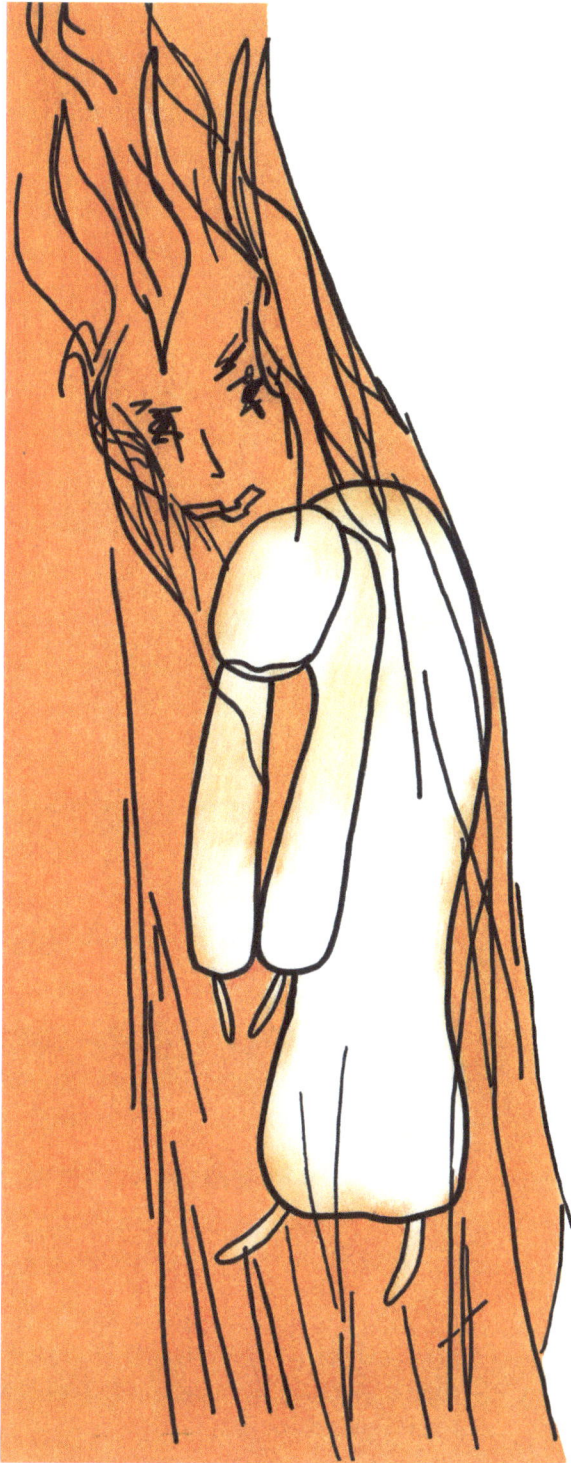

FORWARD THRUST

She had known years
of this pushing
trudging motion
before the actual
cave in
came
and that is why
nobody could fathom
the iniative
it took
to build herself up
into a new person
unless
they themselves
had been there.

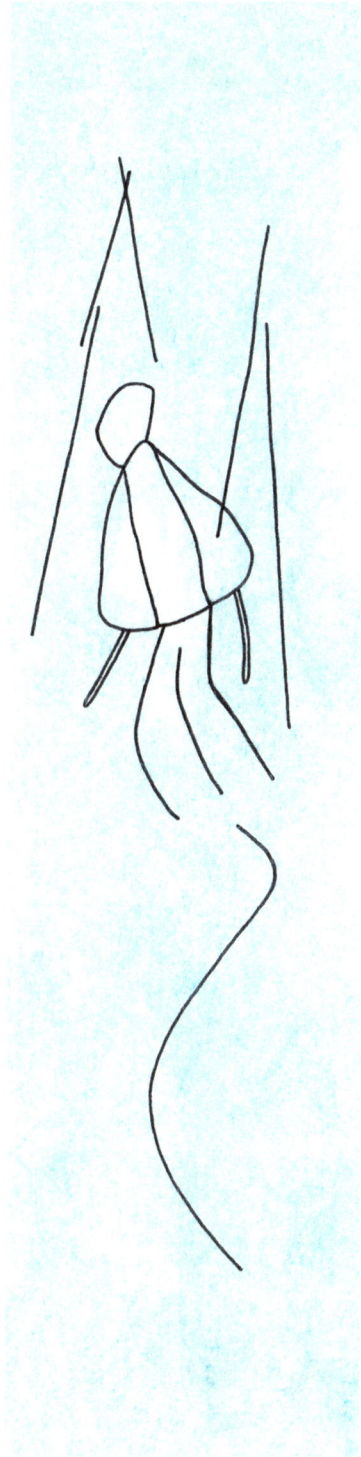

BREAKING DOWN

One day
the wall would collapse
and relief would come
but until then
it required
some kind of a bravery
of heart
to do
what she was doing
and, yet,
in spite of her pushing
she couldn't go on
hiding her limitations
much longer
because
the pressure
was mounting
and her endurance
had come
to an end.

CONSCIENCE

The thorny wanderer
who questioned
not the
hardness
of what
she was doing
but the
rightness
of what
her heart
told her
she had to do.

DETOUR LIVING

If it is the wild nature
of a bull
you carry
then say
it is the wild nature
of a bull.
In this way
you will not deceive yourself
in your thinking
and your emotions
which are the accurate gage
of how you feel
will register
what is true
and right for you.
Living this way
you will look
to the winding road
and say to it...
Anything is beautiful
when you start
believing in it —
even you,
oh road of impossible direction,
even you!

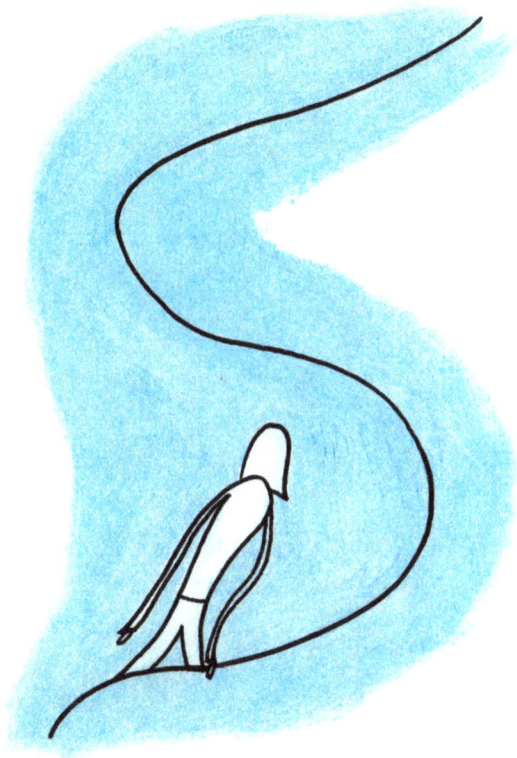

HEALING TRAUMA

She was not
the type
of a person
to lean on anyone
and yet,
when the trauma
occurred,
she needed
all the support
she could get.
As it was,
she had wanted
to retain
her gentleness
but without a fight
hostility,
she said,
was something
that could
have ravaged her.

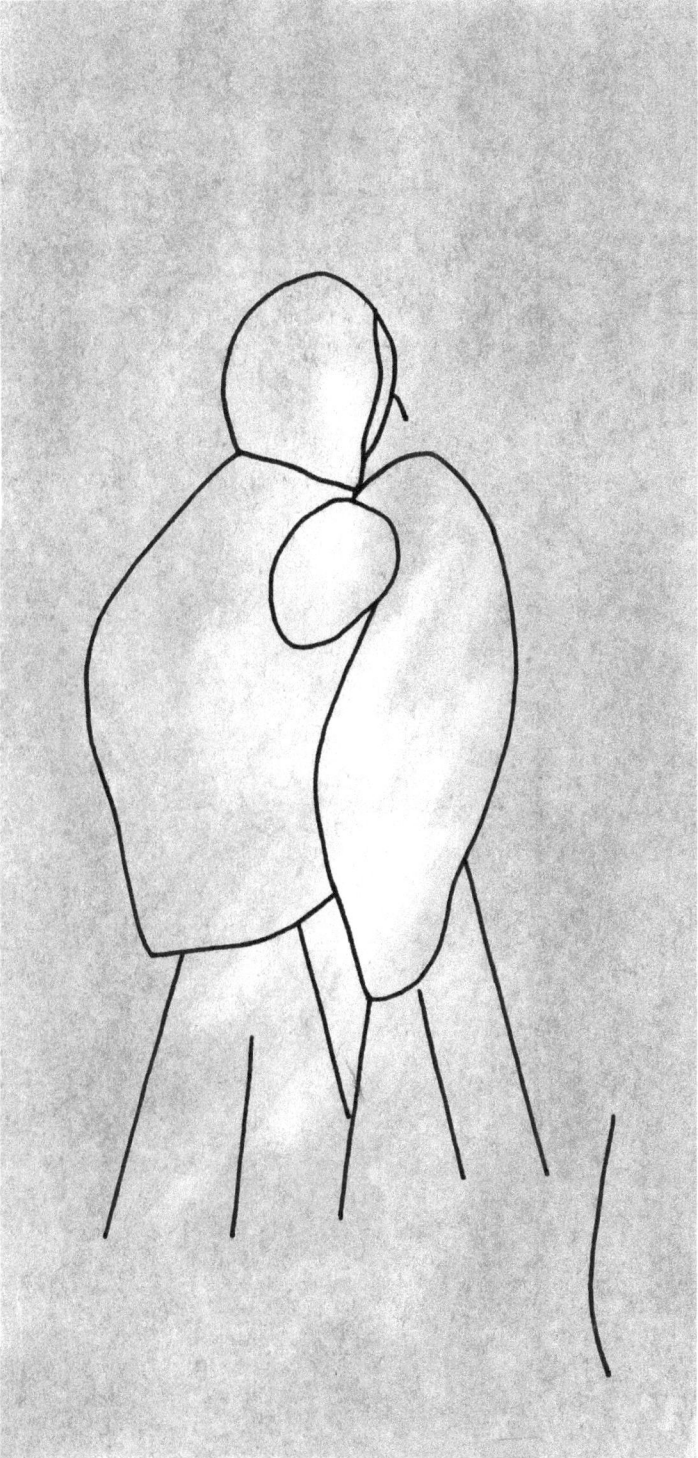

SPIRITUAL HUNGER

You never were satisfied
with what the world
could give you
were you?
It was
like you said-
trying to be fashionable
when you knew
very well
the clothing
never would fit.
Is it any wonder, then,
that you were driven
heart, body,
mind and soul
to what
would one day be
the fulfillment
of these
insatiable desires.

I met a friend
who reminded me
of what I once was
and I said to her —
Fears are like albatrosses
hanging around your neck.
You've got to get rid of them
to be free.
And she in answer
said to me —
What is an albatross?
To which I replied —
Albatrosses, friend,
are those fences
which you and I
build up around our ego.
They are that part of us
we do not accept
and that we therefore feel
we must hide from anyone
who might suspect
that we are deficient.
And so it is, friend,
we walk crippled
by the very structures we create
not realizing
that we are to blame
for much of the evil
in our society.

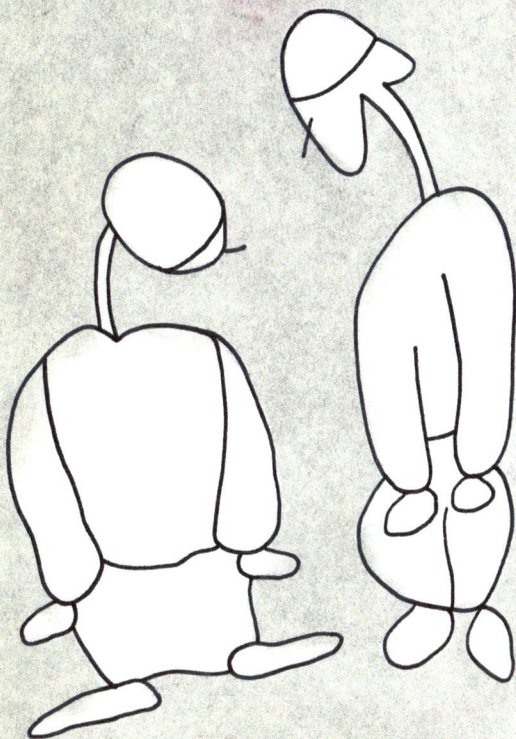

SEASON OF CONFLICT

After she had forgotten
about the dilemma
that made her
as old
as a knarled tree
she returned to say
that the possession
of hope
was with her
but that up until now
it was the conflict
of a changing personality
that had harassed her.

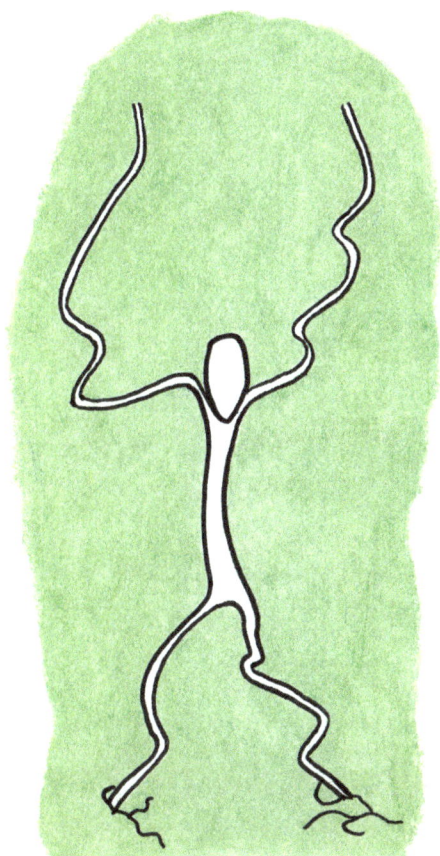

PATIENT WRESTLER

We may say
if only we could see
the lily of ourselves
ahead of time
we would subject ourselves
to the blade
of this Digger
but the truth is
that we cannot bear
to see the hard quality
of our beauty
all at once
and, so,
we must do
what everyone must do
wrestle
patiently
with the mystery
of its unfolding.

MOUNTAIN HOPE

Demolish the lie
and, then,
you will be able to say –
sworded belief
I have paid for you
often enough
to be able to walk through
these mountains of hope –
that was the message
of the treacherous beauty
running through
the devious heart
of this woman
and out of such treachery,
she said,
the honesty would come.

FUTURE OPTIMIST

She knew
that some people walk
more surely through life
than others
and, even though,
she had been detained
by the pessimism
of her early childhood
it was only right now
that she should move
through it
with the true
kind of optimism
she had always
been striving for.

TRUEST FRIEND

Sometimes
her beloved
was as gentle
as a soft cloud
rolling down a mountain
and sometimes he wasn't
but in this friend
she had found
a truth
and a confidentiality
unparalleled
a truth
and a confidentiality
that would make her
want to return to him
again and again.

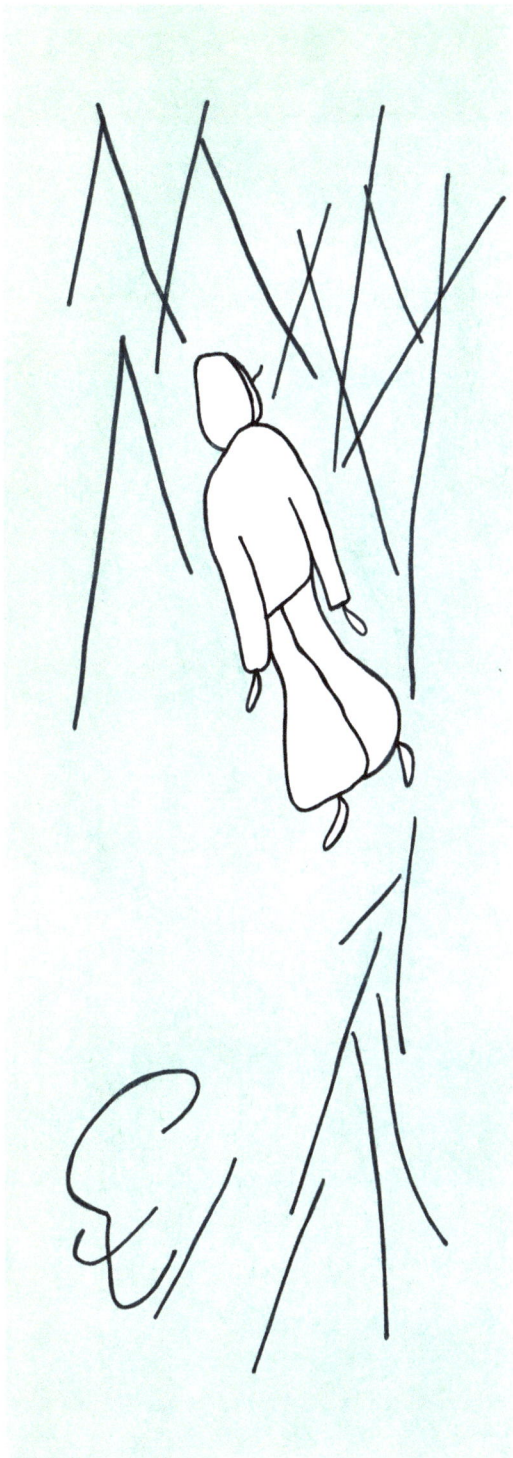

THE DESIRED CALM

She paid heavily
for the calm heart
that was in her now,
and said,
if the violent wind
had subsided
it was because
the danger was over
and that whatever
in her
was to be severed
was severed.

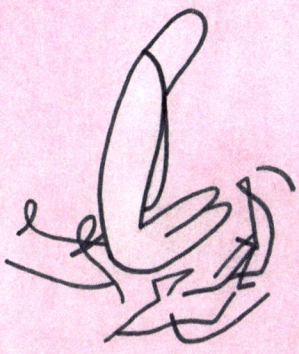

HILL CLIMBER

At times
she felt like evading
the unknown territory
of her heart
because
what transpired there
was anything but pleasant
and, so,
she would push it down
out of sight
until it would reappear again.
Then she would say
to the whole world
let me soar
like a bird
and somehow
she knew
she could do it
but first of all
there were these hills
to contend with.

THE DAGGERED TRUTH

Facing up
to the truth
about herself
was the most horrible revelation
she could think of
and, yet,
if it took
this kind
of self exposure
to make her a better person
she would submit
to the dagger
of it
how ever
many times
that would be.

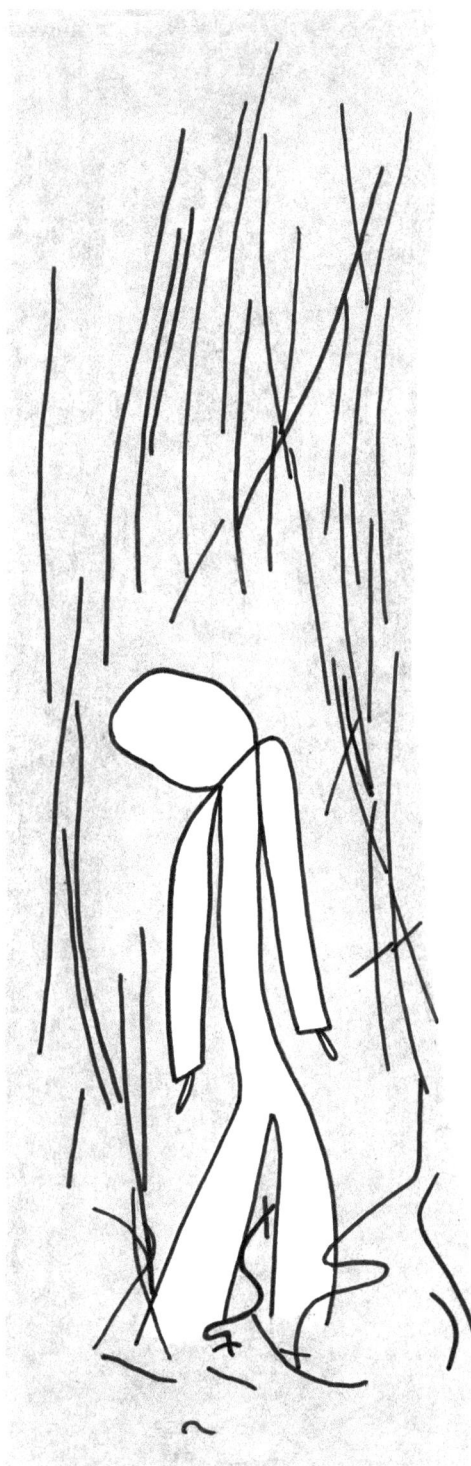

IN RETROSPECT

She looked back
once more
but, only,
because she knew
she would never return
to that place
of unrest
again.
It was too vulnerable
living there,
she said,
and there was no reason
for her
to repeat the agony
if she didn't have to.

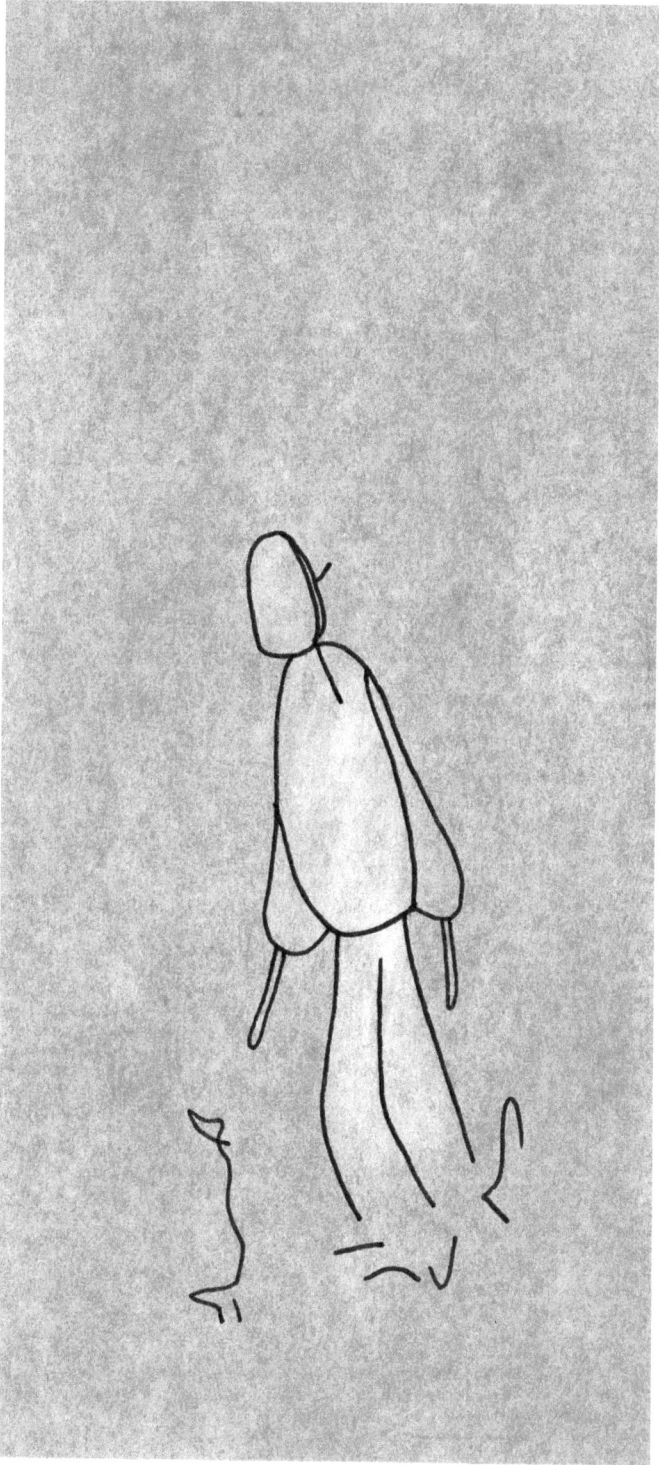

NEW PERSPECTIVES

The venture was on
and she liked
what was happening
to her.
Already
it seemed
as if she were going
somewhere worthwhile
and it wasn't
the same old boredom,
she said,
that it used to be
because now
she was beginning
to live
out of a new set
of standards
and that in itself
was making a difference.

STEPPING FORWARD

It was good
that the hills
of these
past memories
were behind
her now
because
she was walking
into a future
that would not
let her be
saddened
by them.

SEASON OF HOPE

At last
the windy trail
gave way
and she found herself
in a clearing
a space
where she didn't
have to be
disillusioned

anymore.
Gone now
was the unsettled mind
of a twisted person
and in its place
a serenity
she could count on.

Eileen Curteis, ssa

Photograph by
Barbara Benedetti

ABOUT THE AUTHOR

For the last 27 years, Eileen Curteis, a Sister of Saint Ann, has been involved in the Reiki Healing Ministry, a revered eastern healing art that she combines with her Christian heritage of healing. A former teacher, principal and educator for 27 years, Eileen shares that her greatest passion now lies in her healing ministry and in the literary arts. She has authored thirteen books to date and has become an accomplished poet, artist, and writer, as well as being a producer of seven CDs and three films. She lives in Victoria, BC.

You can view Eileen's books, CDs, and DVDs at: www.BooksofExcellence.com

www.ingramcontent.com/pod-product-compliance
Lightning Source LLC
Chambersburg PA
CBHW051237090426
42742CB00001B/3